Riparian Condition Assessments for the Pecos River and Lower Glorieta Creek

Pecos National Historical Park, New Mexico

Natural Resource Report NPS/NRSS/WRD/NRR—2011/422

Joel Wagner

National Park Service
Water Resources Division
P.O. Box 25287
Denver, Colorado 80225

Michael Martin

National Park Service
Water Resources Division
1201 Oakridge Drive, Suite 250
Fort Collins, Colorado 80525

July 2011

U.S. Department of the Interior
National Park Service
Natural Resource Stewardship and Science
Fort Collins, Colorado

The National Park Service, Natural Resource Stewardship and Science office in Fort Collins, Colorado publishes a range of reports that address natural resource topics of interest and applicability to a broad audience in the National Park Service and others in natural resource management, including scientists, conservation and environmental constituencies, and the public.

The Natural Resource Report Series is used to disseminate high-priority, current natural resource management information with managerial application. The series targets a general, diverse audience, and may contain NPS policy considerations or address sensitive issues of management applicability.

All manuscripts in the series receive the appropriate level of peer review to ensure that the information is scientifically credible, technically accurate, appropriately written for the intended audience, and designed and published in a professional manner. This report received formal peer review by subject-matter experts who were not directly involved in the collection, analysis, or reporting of the data, and whose background and expertise put them on par technically and scientifically with the authors of the information.

Views, statements, findings, conclusions, recommendations, and data in this report do not necessarily reflect views and policies of the National Park Service, U.S. Department of the Interior. Mention of trade names or commercial products does not constitute endorsement or recommendation for use by the U.S. Government.

This report is available from the Natural Resource Publications Management website (http://www.nature.nps.gov/publications/nrpm/). Please cite this publication as:

Wagner, J. and M. Martin. 2011. Riparian condition assessments for the Pecos River and lower Glorieta Creek: Pecos National Historical Park, New Mexico. Natural Resource Report NPS/NRSS/WRD/NRR—2011/422. National Park Service, Fort Collins, Colorado.

NPS 430/108149, July 2011

Contents

Figures

Appendices

Executive Summary

This report presents the results of riparian condition assessments conducted during July 6-8, 2010 on the Pecos River and lower Glorieta Creek within Pecos National Historical Park, New Mexico. These assessments were intended to inform the Natural Resource Condition Assessment and the Resource Stewardship Strategy now being prepared for the park. We used methods described in "A User Guide to Assessing the Proper Functioning Condition and the Supporting Science for Lotic Areas" (USDI 1998) to evaluate 17 hydrology, vegetation, soil and geomorphology elements for three assessment reaches on the Pecos River and one reach on lower Glorieta Creek. We then rated the reaches as being in "proper functioning," "functional at-risk" or "nonfunctional" condition. Riparian condition checklists and supporting notes prepared for all assessment reaches are provided in the appendices.

All three Pecos River reaches are in "proper functioning condition" (highest possible rating). However, the lower Glorieta Creek reach was rated "functional – at risk with a downward trend" due to the man-made levee adjacent to the stream channel. The levee constrains the channel to an artificially narrow corridor, which limits the potential size, structural complexity, and habitat value of this riparian system. In addition, flood flows have the potential to erode through the levee and deposit excessive sediment into the newly restored wetlands east and north of the levee, and into downstream aquatic habitats. We strongly recommend removal of the remaining levee to complete the lower Glorieta Creek restoration (i.e., connect the restored riparian-wetland area to the stream corridor), allow the riparian system to reach its full potential for habitat size, diversity, and quality, and eliminate the threat of excessive sediment deposition in aquatic systems.

Acknowledgments

We thank Dan Jacobs, Chief of Natural Resource Management and Visitor Protection for Pecos NHP, for requesting and coordinating this technical assistance and for arranging our accommodations. Dan assisted us greatly by giving guidance and context for our work and by providing information on the watershed land use history, locations of river/stream access points, stressors and threats (including dams and diversions), fire history, beaver activity, livestock grazing history and other factors that may be influencing channel and floodplain characteristics and processes. Yvonne Chauvin, botanist with the New Mexico Natural Heritage Program, was a very valuable member of the riparian assessment team. She provided excellent assistance with plant identification and riparian plant ecology for the area, and proved to be an enjoyable and fearless companion when a thunderstorm turned one of our field days into a memorable adventure.

We also thank Steve Monroe, hydrologist, NPS Southern Colorado Plateau I&M Network, Mark Wondzell, hydrologist, NPS Water Resources Division and Dean Tucker, Acting Chief, Planning and Evaluation Branch, NPS Water Resources Division for their participation in the peer review process for this report. Their comments were on target and helped us improve this final version.

Introduction

Pecos National Historical Park (PECO) is a 6,669-acre unit of the National Park System, located in the southern Sangre de Cristo Mountains near the town of Pecos, New Mexico (Figure 1). The park preserves 12,000 years of history including Pecos Pueblo and Spanish Mission ruins, Santa Fe Trail sites, and the site of the Civil War Battle of Glorieta Pass. These historical resources lie amidst piñon, juniper, and pine woodlands, the Pecos River, and other natural and cultural features of the park.

Under the direction of the National Park Service's Water Resources Division (WRD) and PECO, the University of New Mexico is conducting a Natural Resource Condition Assessment (NRCA) for the park. The assessment evaluates and reports on current conditions, critical data gaps, and selected threat and stressor influences relative to important park natural resources, including the park's riparian areas. Although previous studies of the Pecos River within PECO have surveyed and mapped the vegetation communities of the riparian corridor (Muldavin 1991) and collected baseline vegetation data suitable for assessing change over time (Gage and Cooper 2010), these studies were not designed to provide summary determinations regarding overall riparian "functional condition" or "ecological health." Therefore, park staff and the WRD coordinator for the NRCA Program (Jeff Albright) asked us to conduct a riparian condition assessment for the Pecos River that could be used to inform the ongoing NRCA project for PECO. During our site visit, park staff asked us to also assess the condition of lower Glorieta Creek. Field work for both riparian condition assessments was conducted during July 6-8, 2010.

PECO is also developing a Resource Stewardship Strategy (RSS) for the park in cooperation with Colorado State University, WRD and others. An RSS serves as a strategic planning link between the desired conditions identified in a park's General Management Plan and the actions that are needed to achieve them. Through the RSS process, parks identify indicators of resource condition, establish targets for each indicator, assess current indicator values, analyze the difference (if any) between current conditions and desired conditions, and develop comprehensive strategies to achieve or maintain desired conditions. Because of the link between our riparian assessments and the need for resource condition information and indicators for the RSS, the results presented in this report were provided to the RSS team through the authors' participation in a July 9, 2010 RSS workshop at the park and through a September 16, 2010 WRD trip report.

Methods

We started the assessment process by examining historic (1958, 1982) and recent (2009) aerial photography for the park, stage and discharge records for the Pecos River near Pecos, NM (USGS station 08378500), USGS 7.5 minute topographic maps for the area and previous studies of the Pecos River riparian zone (Muldavin 1991, Gage and Cooper 2010). We were also very familiar with the lower Glorieta Creek riparian area, having participated in the restoration of lower Glorieta Creek in 1999-2000.

When we arrived at the park, we interviewed Dan Jacobs (Chief of Natural Resource Management and Visitor Protection) regarding watershed land use history, locations of river/stream access points, stressors and threats (including dams and diversions), fire history, beaver activity and other factors that may be influencing channel and floodplain characteristics and processes. He described a long history of livestock grazing in the watershed and some flow concentration and sediment delivery associated with highway construction. We then asked if there were any relatively unimpacted "reference reaches" in this same landscape setting that we could use to calibrate our findings within the park. Dan said there has been no livestock grazing in the park for the last 20 years, and so the park's riparian systems are the least impacted in the area.

Based on this initial research, we divided the Pecos River corridor into three roughly equal-length assessment reaches (Figure 2), each of which exhibits fairly consistent morphological characteristics along its length. These reaches also coincide with the three, one-mile long fishing "beats" that the park uses for managing public fishing on the Pecos River. For lower Glorieta Creek, we evaluated a single 0.5 mile reach extending from the Highway 63 Bridge down to the lower end of the man-made levee that parallels the creek (Figure 2). Figures 3-5 and 7 are photo enlargements of the individual assessment reaches, with some key features identified.

We used "A User Guide to Assessing the Proper Functioning Condition and the Supporting Science for Lotic Areas" (USDI 1998) to evaluate the condition of the Pecos River and lower Glorieta Creek riparian zones. For this method, the "proper functioning condition" (PFC) of a riparian area refers to the stability of the physical system, which in turn is dictated by the interaction of geology, soil, water, and vegetation. A riparian area in PFC is in dynamic equilibrium with its streamflow forces and channel processes. The system adjusts to handle larger runoff events with limited change in channel characteristics and associated riparian-wetland plant communities. (This limited change, such as some cutbank erosion and point bar expansion in stream meanders, is within the context of natural stream evolution and provides new geomorphic features for riparian-wetland vegetation recruitment.) Because of this resiliency, riparian areas in PFC can maintain aquatic habitat, water quality enhancement, and other important ecosystem functions, even after larger storms. In contrast, nonfunctional systems in the same storms might exhibit excessive erosion and sediment loading, loss of aquatic and wetland habitat, and so on.

For this method, an interdisciplinary team of technical experts evaluates 17 hydrologic, vegetation, soil and geomorphology elements for each riparian assessment area. Technical guidance for analyzing these elements is provided in the PFC "user guide" referenced above. The team evaluates and scores all 17 elements on the data sheets, and supports the decisions with detailed technical notes. After the individual elements have been assessed, the team assigns one of the following three summary ratings to a site:

"Proper Functioning Condition": Streams and associated riparian areas are functioning properly when adequate vegetation, landform, or large woody debris is present to:

1. Dissipate stream energy associated with high waterflows, thereby reducing erosion and improving water quality;
2. filter sediment, capture bedload, and aid floodplain development;
3. improve floodwater retention and groundwater recharge;
4. develop root masses that stabilize stream banks against cutting action;

2

5. develop diverse ponding and channel characteristics to provide habitat and the water depths, durations, temperature regimes, and substrates necessary for fish production, waterfowl breeding, and other uses; and
6. support greater biodiversity.

"Functional-At Risk": These riparian areas are in functional condition, but an existing soil, water, vegetation, or related attribute makes them susceptible to degradation. For example, a stream reach may exhibit attributes of a properly functioning riparian system, but it may be poised to suffer severe erosion during a large storm in the future due to likely migration of a headcut or increased runoff associated with recent urbanization in the watershed. When this rating is assigned to a stream reach, then its "trend" toward or away from PFC is assessed.

"Nonfunctional": These are riparian areas that clearly are not providing adequate vegetation, landform, or large woody debris to dissipate stream energy associated with high flows, and thus are not reducing erosion, improving water quality, sustaining desirable channel and riparian habitat characteristics, and so on as described in the PFC definition. The absence of certain physical attributes such as a floodplain where one should exist is an indicator of nonfunctioning conditions.

Data sheets showing the results of the assessments and detailed supporting notes are provided in Appendices 1-4 of this report.

Assessment Reach Results and Discussion

Pecos River Reach #1: Northern park boundary to confluence with Glorieta Creek

Rating: Proper Functioning Condition

Figure 3 is an aerial photograph of this river reach, with some key features identified. Channel sinuosity, width/depth ratio, and gradient in this reach are in balance with the landscape setting. The channel and floodplain are able to pass the water and sediment being delivered by the watershed without excessive erosion or deposition (watershed is not contributing to riparian-wetland degradation). The northernmost meander has a secondary channel that may be the result of past channel modifications to provide irrigation water for the apple orchard on the adjacent terrace. Regardless of origin, this feature does not threaten the stability of this riparian reach.

The relatively narrow, low terraces adjacent to the straight channel segments (cover photo) and the point bars in the meander bends are inundated in relatively frequent flood events. The higher second terraces evident throughout the reach do not experience such frequent flooding, though apparently even-aged stands of cottonwood trees (average of about 15" dbh, perhaps 30-40 years old) indicate that they are flooded during much larger (but less frequent) runoff events. Slight erosion on cutbanks and associated point bar development within alluvium are consistent with expected lateral channel migration in this system. In river segments where bedrock outcrops control lateral migration on the outside of meander bends, the riparian zones have likely reached their potential lateral extent.

On the active floodplain (lowest terraces and point bars), sandbar willow _(Salix exigua)_ dominates the woody community and is spreading clonally to provide significant recruitment. Scattered young strapleaf willows _(Salix ligulifolia)_, dewystem willows _(Salix irrorata)_, narrowleaf cottonwoods _(Populus angustifolia)_, Rocky Mountain junipers _(Juniperus scopulorum)_ and green ashes _(Fraxinus pennsylvanica)_ are also establishing and contributing to woody species diversity in this zone. Some terraces have been cleared of Rocky Mountain junipers. The dense canopy and forest floor litter of the junipers act to protect the underlying soil from erosion. Removal of junipers may increase soil erosion by exposing the ground surface to the high-energy impact of direct rainfall.

Herbaceous wetland species such as reed-canary grass _(Phalaris arundinacea)_, spikerush _(Eleocharis sp.)_ and arctic rush _(Juncus arcticus)_ dominate the herbaceous component of the active floodplain and appear to be healthy and spreading. These native riparian-wetland species provide adequate root masses and above ground biomass to protect riverbanks from excessive erosion, dissipate energy during flood flows, filter sediment, provide habitat diversity, moderate stream temperatures, and provide other desirable riparian-wetland functions.

On the second terraces, narrowleaf cottonwoods dominate the tree and shrub layers and are spreading clonally to provide significant recruitment. (A few cottonwoods showed evidence of beaver herbivory, but there was no evidence of dam building within the reach.) Gambel oak is also well-represented and adds diversity to this community. These native species support

5

important riparian functions such as dissipation of flood energy, capture of sediment, sources of woody debris, and habitat diversity. Grass species cover on these terraces is almost entirely non-native (e.g., smooth brome *(Bromus inermis)* and tall fescue *(Festuca arundinacea)).*

Summary and conclusions: The PFC Checklist for this reach (Appendix 1) shows that all applicable elements were rated positively, indicating to the team that the reach is in Proper Functioning Condition. "Remarks" on the back of the checklist page provide the team's justifications for many of the individual checklist responses. The park staff also asked us to record any observations of impacts associated with fishing access during our assessments. We did not observe any evidence of trailing, localized vegetation trampling, bank destabilization or trash associated with fishing access.

Pecos River Reach #2: Confluence with Glorieta Creek south to abandoned iron bridge

Rating: Proper Functioning Condition

Figure 4 is an aerial photograph of this river reach, with some key features identified. The overall morphology of this reach (e.g., sinuosity, gradient, channel form) is controlled by shallow bedrock (base level control) and bedrock outcrops that limit lateral migration in some segments. Within that context, channel sinuosity, width/depth ratio, and gradient are in balance with this landscape setting. The channel and floodplain are able to pass the water and sediment being delivered by the watershed without excessive erosion or deposition (watershed is not contributing to riparian-wetland degradation).

The relatively narrow, low terraces adjacent to the straighter channel segments and the point bars in the meander bends are inundated in relatively frequent flood events. The higher second terraces evident throughout the reach do not experience such frequent flooding, though apparently even-aged cottonwood stands indicate that they are flooded during much larger (but less frequent) runoff events. Slight erosion on cutbanks and associated point bar development within alluvium are consistent with expected lateral channel migration in this system. In river segments where bedrock outcrops control lateral migration on the outside of meander bends, the riparian zones have likely reached their potential lateral extent. In other segments these zones may still be widening.

On the lowest terraces and point bars, sandbar willow dominates the woody riparian shrub community and is spreading clonally to provide significant recruitment. Scattered young thinleaf alders *(Alnus incana* ssp. *tenuifolia)*, strapleaf willows, peachleaf willows *(Salix amygdaloides),* Woods' roses *(Rosa woodsii)* and narrowleaf cottonwoods are also establishing and adding diversity to this community. Reed-canary grass and spikerush commonly form dense mats on wetter sites of the lower terraces/point bars. A Huron green orchid *(Platanthera huronensis)* was found in one low terrace site. These native riparian-wetland species provide adequate root masses and above ground biomass to protect riverbanks from excessive erosion, dissipate energy during flood flows, filter sediment, provide habitat diversity, moderate stream temperatures and provide other desirable riparian-wetland functions.

On the 2nd terraces, narrowleaf cottonwoods dominate the tree and shrub layers, and are spreading clonally to provide significant recruitment. Other woody riparian species adding diversity to this community include Rocky Mountain juniper and box-elder *(Acer negundo)*. These native species support important riparian functions such as dissipation of flood energy, capture of sediment, sources of woody debris, and habitat diversity. Grass cover on the second terraces is almost entirely non-native, including smooth brome, Kentucky bluegrass *(Poa pratensis)*, and tall fescue.

Summary and conclusions: The PFC Checklist for this river reach (Appendix 2) shows that all applicable elements were rated positively, indicating to the team that the reach is in Proper Functioning Condition. "Remarks" on the back of the checklist page provide the team's justifications for many of the individual checklist responses. We did not observe any evidence of trailing, localized vegetation trampling, bank destabilization or trash associated with fishing access.

Pecos River Reach #3: Abandoned iron bridge to southern park boundary

Rating: Proper Functioning Condition

Figure 5 is an aerial photograph of this river reach, with some key features identified. The overall morphology of this reach (e.g., sinuosity, gradient, channel form) is controlled by substantial shallow bedrock (base level control) and bedrock outcrops that limit lateral migration in some segments. However, point bars are better developed here (Figure 6) than on reaches 1 and 2, being larger in width and area and having more diverse topographic structure (including oxbows and overflow channels). This topographic complexity contributes to the more diverse wetland-riparian vegetation communities discussed below. Within that context, channel sinuosity, width/depth ratio, and gradient are in balance with this landscape setting. The channel and floodplain are able to pass the water and sediment being delivered by the watershed without excessive erosion or deposition (watershed is not contributing to riparian-wetland degradation).

The relatively narrow, low terraces adjacent to the straighter channel segments and the point bars in the meander bends are inundated in relatively frequent flood events. The higher second terraces evident throughout the reach do not experience such frequent flooding, though cottonwood stands of at least two age classes indicate that they are flooded during much larger (but less frequent) runoff events. Slight erosion on cutbanks and associated point bar development within alluvium are consistent with expected lateral channel migration in this system. In river segments where bedrock outcrops control lateral migration on the outside of meander bends, the riparian zones have likely reached their potential lateral extent. In other segments these zones may still be widening.

On the lowest terraces and point bars (active floodplain), sandbar willow dominates the woody riparian shrub community and is spreading clonally to provide significant recruitment. Thinleaf alders, strapleaf willows, peachleaf willows, narrowleaf cottonwoods and a few Rio Grande cottonwoods *(Populus deltoides* ssp. *wislizeni)* have also established and are adding diversity to this community. These additional woody species are still scattered among the more dominant sandbar willows, but they are more common here than in reaches 1 and 2. Saplings of both cottonwood species are present, especially on active floodplain features with structural complexity. Through much of the reach, reed-canary grass and spikerush are the dominant herbaceous wetland species within the active floodplain. However, the greater diversity of floodplain structural components on the large point bars also support dense patches of arctic rush, Nebraska sedge *(Carex nebrascensis),* cattail *(Typha* sp.*)*, redtop *(Agrostis gigantea),* and several other *Carex* and *Juncus* species. Huron green orchids were also observed in this zone. These native riparian-wetland species provide adequate root masses and above ground biomass to protect riverbanks from excessive erosion, dissipate energy during flood flows, filter sediment, provide habitat diversity, moderate stream temperatures and provide other desirable riparian-wetland functions. Patches of the noxious weed teasel *(Dipsacus* sp.) were observed in some low terrace and point bar locations.

On the second terraces, narrowleaf cottonwoods dominate the woody riparian communities and they are spreading clonally to provide significant recruitment. There are some older, decadent cottonwood trees, but these are relatively infrequent and did not raise concerns for the team regarding any anthropogenic cause. Box-elder is more common on terraces in this reach, but it is not a dominant. These native riparian species support important riparian functions such as dissipation of flood energy, capture of sediment, sources of woody debris, and habitat diversity. As with previous reaches, grass cover on the higher second terraces is almost entirely non-native.

Summary and conclusions: The PFC Checklist for this river reach (Appendix 3) shows that all applicable elements were rated positively, indicating to the team that this reach is in Proper Functioning Condition. "Remarks" on the back of the checklist page provide the team's justifications for many of the individual checklist responses. We did not observe any evidence of trailing, localized vegetation trampling, bank destabilization or trash associated with fishing access. The park staff should consider eradication of highly invasive teasel before it displaces additional native plants.

Glorieta Creek Reach: Highway 63 bridge downstream to lower end of remaining artificial levee (0.5 stream miles below bridge)

Rating: Functional – At Risk (downward trend)

Figure 7 is an aerial photograph of this stream reach, with some key features identified. In the upper two-thirds of this assessment reach, channel sinuosity, width/depth ratio, and gradient are in balance with the landscape setting. However, the lower third of the reach has a substantial artificial levee located very near the left bank of the channel. The levee is a remaining section of the former "upper reservoir" that was built by former land owners in mid 1980s and was left in place as a temporary erosion protection measure during the1999-2000 lower Glorieta Creek restoration project. In this lower segment, the channel is forced to stay within an artificially narrow meander belt between the levee and the high terrace to the south. As a result, the stream gradient steepens due to reduced sinuosity. Nevertheless, our observations indicated that the channel and floodplain are able to pass the water and sediment being delivered by the watershed throughout the entire assessment reach without excessive erosion or deposition.

Two beaver dams and associated ponds were observed in sequence at approximately 0.27 and 0.35 stream miles below the Highway 63 bridge (Figure 7). Both are well-stabilized by riparian shrubs, and both are being actively maintained (we observed an adult beaver in the upper pond). These dams play an important role in maintaining high riparian-wetland water tables in their vicinities during the drier parts of the summer and fall.

The relatively narrow, low terraces adjacent to the straighter channel segments and the point bars in the meander bends are inundated in relatively frequent flood events. The higher second terraces throughout the reach do not experience such frequent flooding, though cottonwood stands of at least two age classes indicate that they are flooded during much larger (but less frequent) runoff events. Slight erosion on cutbanks and associated point bar development within alluvium on the upper two-thirds of the reach are consistent with expected lateral channel migration in this system. However, in the lower third of the reach, the levee constrains the channel to an artificially narrow meander belt, restricts lateral stream migration, and therefore reduces the potential width and structural complexity of the riparian area (Figure 7).

Sandbar willow is the dominant riparian shrub throughout the active floodplain, and it is spreading clonally to provide significant recruitment. Young dewystem willows and both narrowleaf and Rio Grande cottonwoods are also well-represented in this zone, indicating ongoing recruitment for these species as well (Figure 8). These four woody species are also very common within the restored "upper reservoir" area behind the remaining levee segment (Figure 9). All four were planted during the restoration, but there is also substantial new recruitment of all from seed and/or clonal spread. Herbaceous wetland species including arctic rush, spikerush, common three-square *(Schoenoplectus pungens)*, cattail and Nebraska sedge form dense mats within the active floodplain (and within the restored "upper reservoir" shown in Figure 9). These native species provide adequate root masses and above ground biomass to protect streambanks from excessive erosion, dissipate energy during flood flows, filter sediment, provide habitat diversity, moderate stream temperatures and provide other desirable riparian-wetland functions (Figure 8).

Middle-aged trees and saplings of Rio Grande cottonwood provide appropriate age-classes for riparian trees on the second terraces. Scattered narrowleaf cottonwoods are present in the upper part of the reach, but this species becomes more common near the lower end of the levee, and is spreading clonally. These native riparian species support important riparian functions such as dissipation of flood energy, capture of sediment, sources of woody debris, and habitat diversity. Non-native grasses dominating the drier second terraces include tall fescue and Kentucky bluegrass.

Summary and conclusions: The PFC Checklist for this stream reach (Appendix 4) shows that most applicable elements were rated positively, but checklist items 3, 4, and 15 were answered "no." (Remarks on the back of the checklist page provide the team's justifications for individual checklist responses.) These negative responses all relate to the remaining levee in the lower third of the reach, which constrains the channel to an artificially narrow meander belt and restricts lateral stream migration. This constriction limits the potential size and structural complexity of the riparian area, which in turn limits potential habitat values there. Although the levee has been in place for about 25 years, the constricted channel and floodplain appear to be functioning properly in response to large storms. We saw no evidence of the excessive erosion, sediment

9

loading, channel incision, or loss of existing aquatic and wetland habitat that might be expected in a non-functional system, despite the stream corridor constriction.

However, there is an ongoing risk that a large flood could cause the creek to erode a new channel through the upper part of the levee (e.g., at the lower beaver dam location shown in Figure 7) and down through the recently restored wetland-riparian area (Figure 9). The result could be excessive deposition of eroded levee material into the recently restored wetlands and back into the Glorieta Creek channel immediately downstream. We therefore assigned the rating "Functional – At Risk" to this stream reach. The trend is "downward" because the levee will continue to degrade over time, increasing the chance for failure. We strongly recommend removal of the remaining levee to complete the lower Glorieta Creek restoration (i.e., connect the restored wetland area to the stream corridor), allow the riparian system to reach its full potential for habitat size, diversity, and quality, and eliminate the threat of excessive sediment deposition in the restored wetlands or downstream riparian system from this source.

References

Gage, E. and D. Cooper. 2010. (Draft) Final Report: Riparian Baseline Data Collection Prior to Opening River to Fishing Access in Pecos National Historical Park. Department of Forest, Rangeland and Watershed Stewardship, Colorado State University, Fort Collins, CO.

Muldavin, E. 1991. Riparian and Wetlands Survey, Pecos National Historical Park. New Mexico Natural Heritage Program, University of New Mexico, Albuquerque, NM.

U.S. Department of the Interior, Bureau of Land Management. 1998. Riparian Area Management: A User Guide to Assessing Proper Functioning Condition and the Supporting Science for Lotic Areas. TR 1737-15. BLM National Applied Resource Sciences Center. Denver, CO.

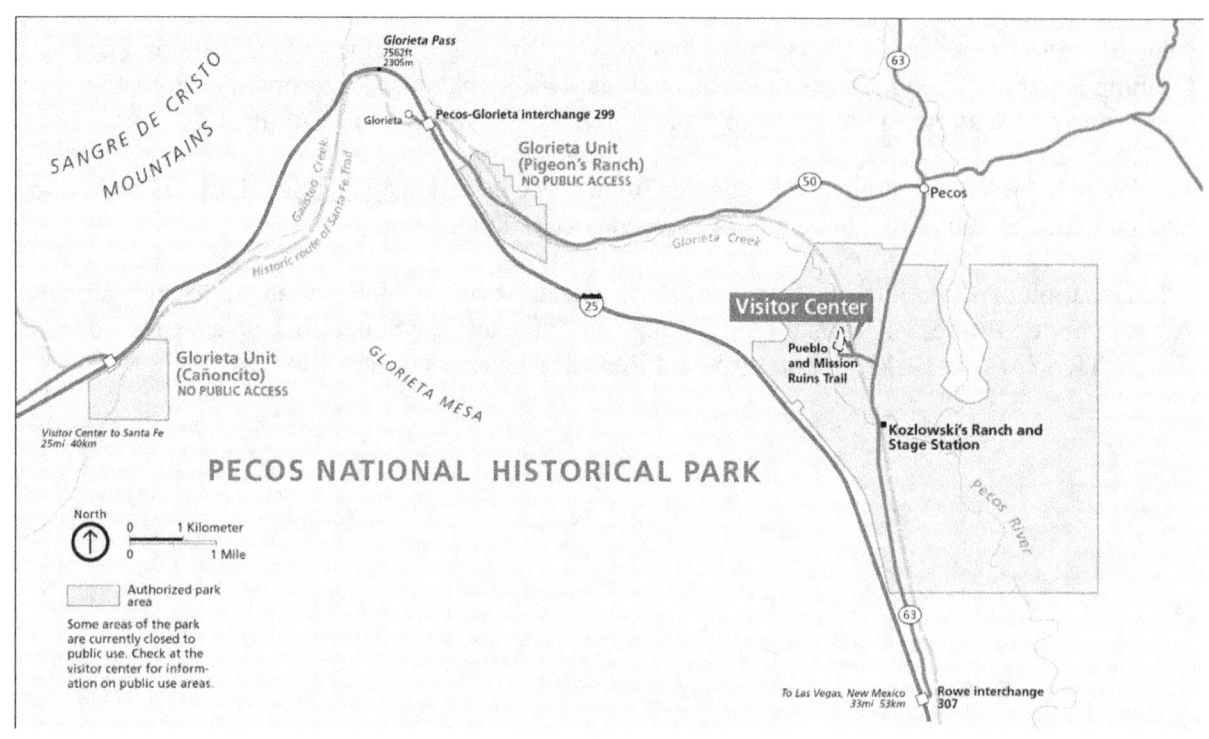

Figure 1. Map of Pecos National Historical Park, New Mexico

Figure 2. Locations of three assessment reaches on the Pecos River (yellow) and one assessment reach on lower Glorieta Creek (white). Individual reaches are shown in Figures 3-5 and 7. Green line is the park boundary. (Photo source: NAIP 2009)

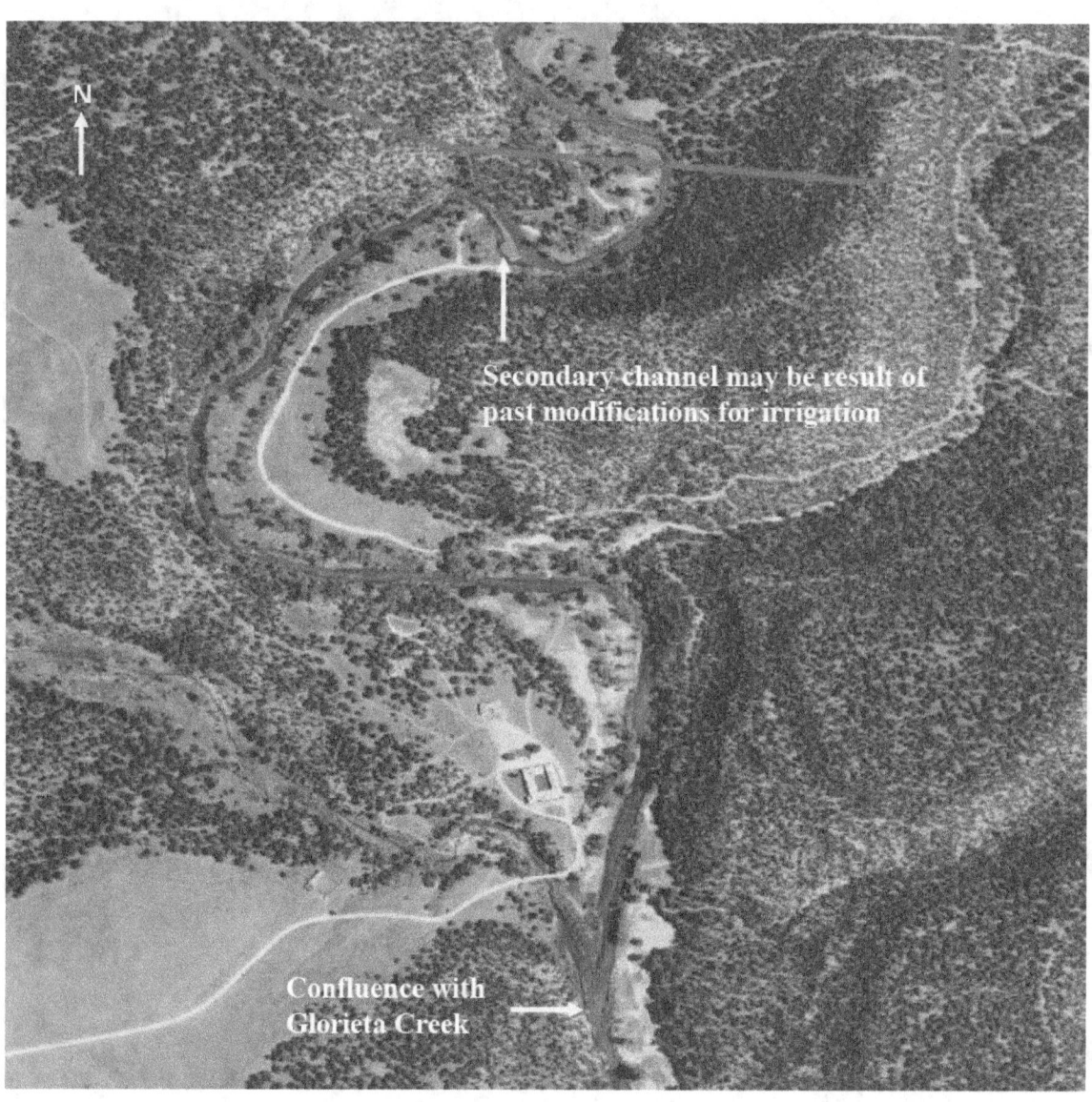

Figure 3. Pecos River Assessment Reach #1 -- northern park boundary (green line) to confluence with Glorieta Creek. (Photo source: NAIP 2009)

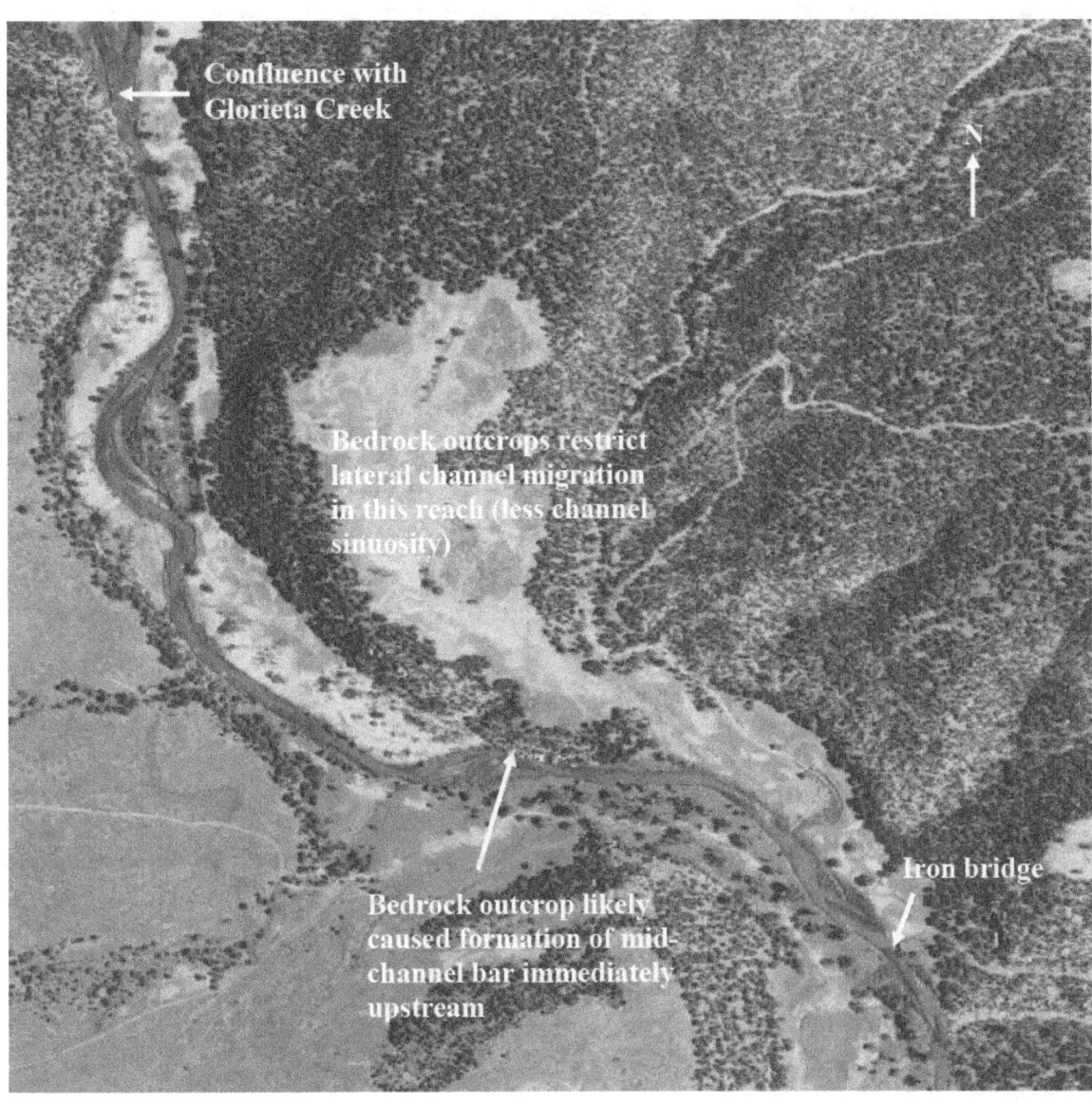

Figure 4. Pecos River Assessment Reach #2 -- confluence with Glorieta Creek south to abandoned iron bridge. (Photo source: NAIP 2009)

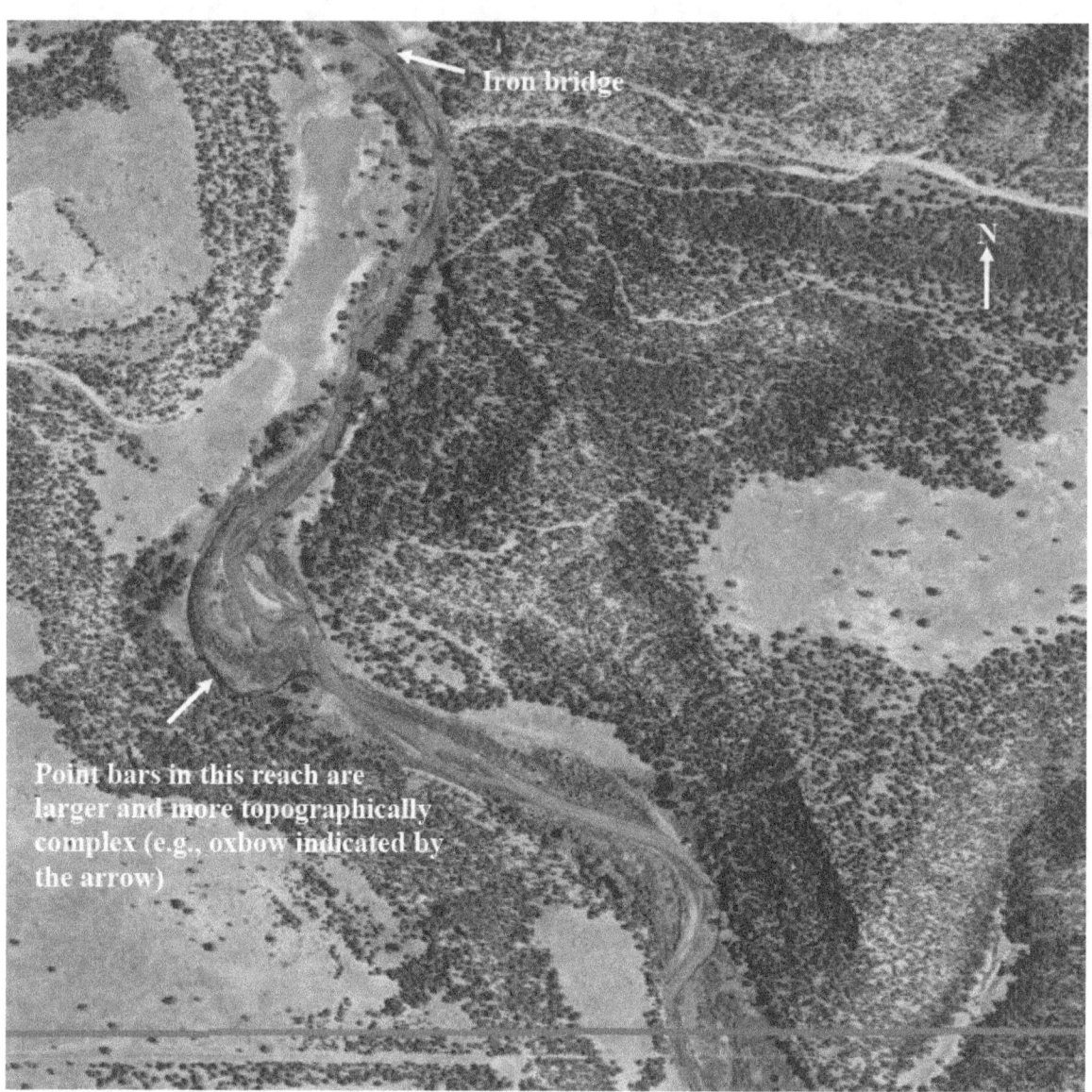

Iron bridge

N

Point bars in this reach are larger and more topographically complex (e.g., oxbow indicated by the arrow)

Figure 5. Pecos River Assessment Reach #3 -- abandoned iron bridge to southern park boundary (green line). (Photo source: NAIP 2009)

Figure 6. Riparian areas on Pecos River Assessment Reach 3 are larger and have more topographic complexity than on reaches 1 and 2, creating more diverse wetland-riparian vegetation communities. (Photo by Michael Martin, NPS-NRSS, Water Resources Division, 2010.)

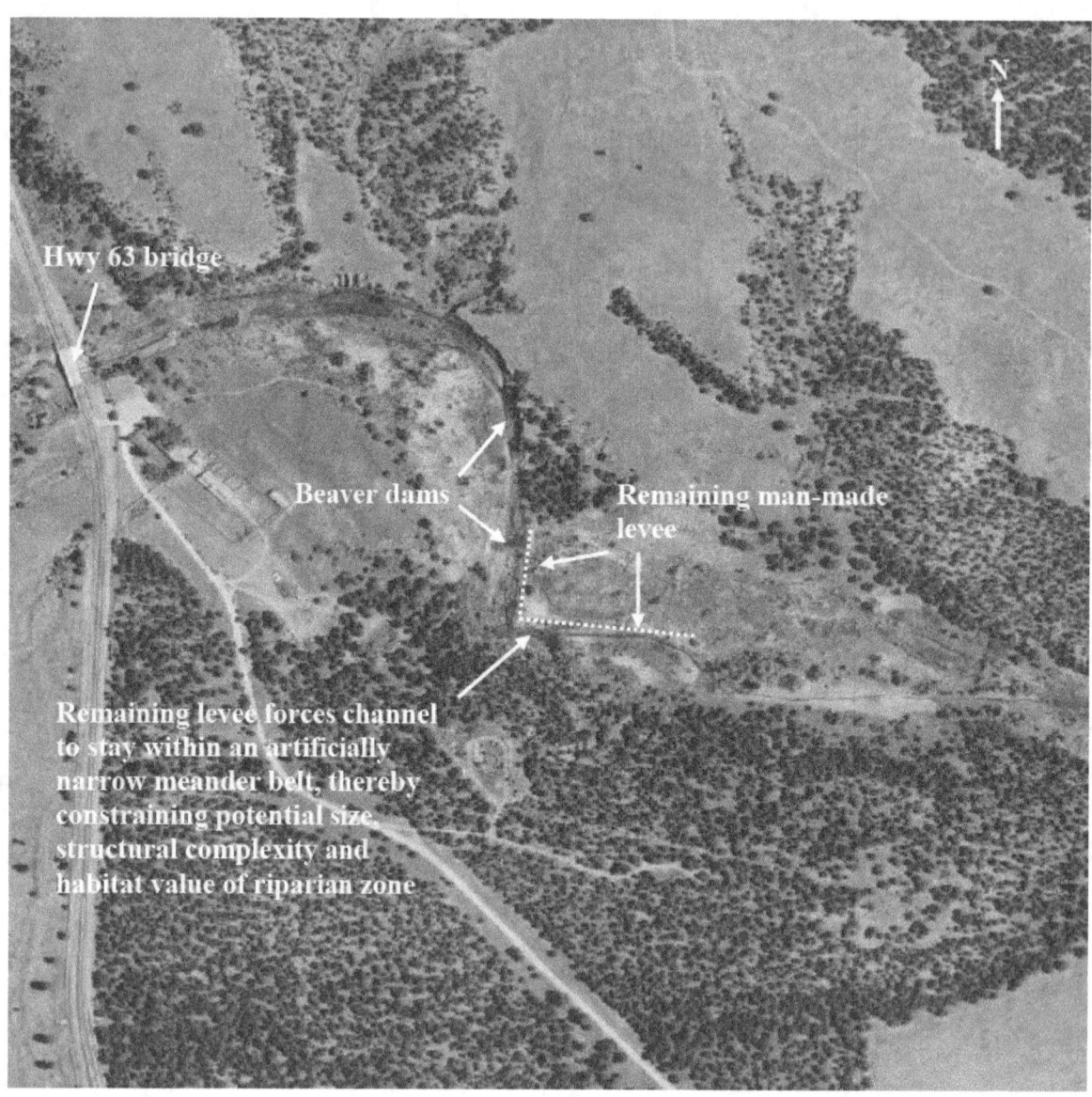

Figure labels on image:

Hwy 63 bridge

Beaver dams

Remaining man-made levee

Remaining levee forces channel to stay within an artificially narrow meander belt, thereby constraining potential size, structural complexity and habitat value of riparian zone

Figure 7. Glorieta Creek Assessment Reach -- Highway 63 bridge downstream to lower end of remaining artificial levee (0.5 stream miles below bridge).   (Photo source: NAIP 2009)

Figure 8. Diverse woody and herbaceous plant communities along the Glorieta Creek reach below the Highway 53 bridge provide adequate root mass and above-ground biomass to protect streambanks from excessive erosion, dissipate flood energy and perform other beneficial riparian-wetland functions. (Photo by Michael Martin, NPS-NRSS, Water Resources Division, 2010.)

Figure 9. Diverse wetland-riparian plant communities are developing within the former reservoirs along lower Glorieta Creek, which were largely restored in 2000. The remaining levee segment (yellow arrow) separating the creek from this portion of the floodplain limits riparian system function and could cause excessive sediment deposition in downstream aquatic habitats. (Photo by Joel Wagner, NPS-NRSS, Water Resources Division, 2007.)

Appendix 1. PFC Riparian System Standard Checklist and Notes for Pecos River Assessment Reach # 1

PFC Lotic (Riparian) Standard Checklist

Name of Riparian Area: ___Pecos River within Pecos NHP___
Date: __7-7-2010__   Segment/Reach ID: _Reach #1 – northern park boundary to confluence_
_with Glorieta Creek___
Miles: _approx. 1 stream mile_   Acres:_____
ID Team Observers: _Joel Wagner, Mike Martin, Yvonne Chauvin_____

Yes	No	N/A	HYDROLOGY
X			1) Floodplain above bankfull is inundated in "relatively frequent" events
		X	2) Where beaver dams are present they are active and stable
X			3) Sinuosity, width/depth ratio, and gradient are in balance with the landscape setting (i.e., landform, geology, and bioclimatic region)
X			4) Riparian-wetland area is widening or has achieved potential extent
X			5) Upland watershed is not contributing to riparian-wetland degradation

Yes	No	N/A	VEGETATION
X			6) There is diverse age-class distribution of riparian-wetland vegetation (recruitment for maintenance/recovery)
X			7) There is diverse composition of riparian-wetland vegetation (for maintenance/recovery)
X			8) Species present indicate maintenance of riparian-wetland soil moisture characteristics
X			9) Streambank vegetation is comprised of those plants or plant communities that have root masses capable of withstanding high-streamflow events
X			10) Riparian-wetland plants exhibit high vigor
X			11) Adequate riparian-wetland vegetative cover is present to protect banks and dissipate energy during high flows
		X	12) Plant communities are an adequate source of coarse and/or large woody material (for maintenance/recovery)

Yes	No	N/A	EROSION/DEPOSITION
X			13) Floodplain and channel characteristics (i.e., rocks, overflow channels, coarse and/or large woody material) are adequate to dissipate energy
X			14) Point bars are revegetating with riparian-wetland vegetation
X			15) Lateral stream movement is associated with natural sinuosity
X			16) System is vertically stable
X			17) Stream is in balance with the water and sediment being supplied by the watershed (i.e., no excessive erosion or deposition)

(Revised 1999)

23

Remarks (numbers correspond to checklist items)

1. Two higher Quaternary terraces do not experience frequent flooding, however, the lowest terraces (which are relatively narrow) and point bars are frequently inundated. Cottonwoods on the 2nd terraces appear even-aged (possibly 30-40 years old) and average approximately 15" dbh. These could have been established during a much larger (and less frequent) spring flood event that accessed the second terraces.

4. Riparian area has reached potential extent in segments with bedrock control on the outside of meander bends. Slight erosion on cutbanks and associated point bar development w/in alluvium is consistent with expected lateral channel migration. Riparian zone is near/at potential extent.

6. On the 2nd terraces, narrow-leaf cottonwoods (*Populus angustifolia*) are spreading clonally to provide significant recruitment. On the active floodplain (lowest terraces and point bars), sandbar willows (*Salix exigua*) are spreading clonally to provide significant recruitment. Scattered young strapleaf willows *(Salix ligulifolia),* dewystem willows *(Salix irrorata)* and cottonwoods are establishing on lower terraces/point bars along this reach. Herbaceous wetland species such as reed-canary grass *(Phalaris arundinacea)* form dense mats in the wetter locations.

7. Woody riparian species cover is dominated by narrow-leaf cottonwood on the 2nd terraces and sandbar willow on the lower terraces/point bars. Gambel oak *(Quercus gambelii)* occurs on the second terraces, and strapleaf willows, dewystem willows, Rocky Mountain junipers *(Juniperus scopulorum)* and green ashes *(Fraxinus pennsylvanica)* are found on lower terraces. (Some terraces have been cleared of Rocky Mountain junipers, which provide dense canopies and substantial forest floor litter. Their removal may increase soil erosion.) Herbaceous species in the active floodplain include reed-canary grass, spikerush *(Eleocharis sp.),* and arctic rush *(Juncus arcticus).* Grass species cover on the 2nd terraces (under middle-aged cottonwoods) is almost entirely non-native (e.g., smooth brome *(Bromus inermis)* and tall fescue *(Festuca arundinacea)).*

15. Sequential cutbank/point bar morphology was observed along the reach, as expected for a functional system in this watershed. Active cut bank erosion coupled with opposing point bar accretion is indicative of vertical stability and riparian system maintenance. (See note #1 below.)

17. No sign of excessive sediment deposition or channel incision.

Summary Determination

Functional Rating: **Trend for Functional – At Risk:**

Proper Functioning Condition ___X___   Upward _____

Functional – At Risk _____   Downward _____

Nonfunctional _____   Not Apparent _____

Notes:

1. Secondary channel evident in the northernmost meander may be result of past channel modification to provide irrigation water for the apple orchard on the adjacent terrace. It doesn't threaten system stability.
2. Observations regarding fishing impacts: No evidence of trailing, localized vegetation trampling, bank destabilization or trash observed.

Are factors contributing to unacceptable conditions outside the control of the manager?

Yes ___   No ___X___

If yes, what are those factors?

___ Flow regulations   ___ Mining activities   ___ Upstream channel conditions

___ Channelization   ___ Road encroachment   ___ Oil field water discharge

___ Augmented flows   ___ Other (specify)

24

Appendix 2. PFC Riparian System Standard Checklist and Notes for Pecos River Assessment Reach # 2

PFC Lotic (Riparian) Standard Checklist

Name of Riparian Area: ___Pecos River within Pecos NHP_____

Date: ___7-7-2010_____ Segment/Reach ID: _Reach #2 – confluence with Glorieta Creek south to abandoned iron bridge_____

Miles: approx. 1 stream mile_____ Acres:_____

ID Team Observers: Joel Wagner, Mike Martin, Yvonne Chauvin_____

Yes	No	N/A	HYDROLOGY
X			1) Floodplain above bankfull is inundated in "relatively frequent" events
		X	2) Where beaver dams are present they are active and stable
X			3) Sinuosity, width/depth ratio, and gradient are in balance with the landscape setting (i.e., landform, geology, and bioclimatic region)
X			4) Riparian-wetland area is widening or has achieved potential extent
X			5) Upland watershed is not contributing to riparian-wetland degradation

Yes	No	N/A	VEGETATION
X			6) There is diverse age-class distribution of riparian-wetland vegetation (recruitment for maintenance/recovery)
X			7) There is diverse composition of riparian-wetland vegetation (for maintenance/recovery)
X			8) Species present indicate maintenance of riparian-wetland soil moisture characteristics
X			9) Streambank vegetation is comprised of those plants or plant communities that have root masses capable of withstanding high-streamflow events
X			10) Riparian-wetland plants exhibit high vigor
X			11) Adequate riparian-wetland vegetative cover is present to protect banks and dissipate energy during high flows
		X	12) Plant communities are an adequate source of coarse and/or large woody material (for maintenance/recovery)

Yes	No	N/A	EROSION/DEPOSITION
X			13) Floodplain and channel characteristics (i.e., rocks, overflow channels, coarse and/or large woody material) are adequate to dissipate energy
X			14) Point bars are revegetating with riparian-wetland vegetation
X			15) Lateral stream movement is associated with natural sinuosity
X			16) System is vertically stable
X			17) Stream is in balance with the water and sediment being supplied by the watershed (i.e., no excessive erosion or deposition)

(Revised 1999)

Remarks (numbers correspond to checklist items)

1. Two higher Quaternary terraces don't experience frequent flooding, however, the lowest terraces (which are relatively narrow) and point bars are frequently inundated. Cottonwoods on 2nd terraces appear even-aged (possibly 30-40 years old) and average approx. 15" dbh. These could have been established during a much larger (less frequent) spring flood that accessed the 2nd terraces.

3. Overall morphology of this reach (e.g., sinuosity, gradient) controlled by shallow bedrock (base level control) and bedrock outcrops that limit lateral migration in some segments.

4. Riparian area has reached potential extent in segments with bedrock control on outside of meander bends. Slight erosion on cutbanks and associated point bar development within alluvium is consistent with expected lateral channel migration and is indicative of vertical stability. Riparian zone is near/at potential extent.

5. No indication of excessive runoff /sediment from upland watershed (see note 1 below.)

6. On the 2nd terraces, narrow-leaf cottonwoods (*Populus angustifolia*) are spreading clonally to provide significant recruitment. On the lowest terraces and point bars, sandbar willows (*Salix exigua*) are spreading clonally to provide significant recruitment. Scattered young thinleaf alders (*Alnus incana* ssp. *tenuifolia*), strapleaf willows *(Salix ligulifolia)*, peachleaf willows *(Salix amygdaloides)*, Woods' roses *(Rosa woodsii)* and cottonwoods are establishing on lower terraces/point bars along this reach. Reed-canary grass (*Phalaris arundinacea*) commonly forms dense mats on wetter sites.

7. Woody riparian species cover on the 2nd terraces is dominated by narrow-leaf cottonwood, with Rocky Mountain juniper *(Juniperus scopulorum)* and box-elder *(Acer negundo)* also present. Sandbar willow dominates the lower terraces/point bars, with scattered thinleaf alders, strapleaf and peachleaf willows, and Woods' roses also present. Dominant herbaceous species on the active floodplain include reed-canary grass and spikerush (*Eleocharis* sp*.)* A Huron green orchid *(Platanthera huronensis)* was found in one low terrace site. Grass cover on the 2nd terraces is almost entirely non-native (e.g., smooth brome *(Bromus inermis),* Kentucky bluegrass *(Poa pratensis),* tall fescue *(Festuca arundinacea)*).

15. See remarks 3. and 4. above.

17. No sign of excessive sediment deposition or channel incision.

Summary Determination

Functional Rating:

Proper Functioning Condition	__X__
Functional – At Risk	_____
Nonfunctional	_____

Trend for Functional – At Risk:

Upward	_____
Downward	_____
Not Apparent	_____

Notes:

1. Thick litter layer beneath Junipers protects against upland soil erosion by reducing raindrop impact, increasing infiltration, and reducing overland flow and rill erosion.

2. <u>Observations regarding fishing impacts</u>: No evidence of trailing, localized vegetation trampling, bank destabilization or trash observed.

Are factors contributing to unacceptable conditions outside the control of the manager?
Yes ___ No __X__

If yes, what are those factors?

___ Flow regulations	___ Mining activities	___ Upstream channel conditions
___ Channelization	___ Road encroachment	___ Oil field water discharge
___ Augmented flows	___ Other (specify)	

Appendix 3. PFC Riparian System Standard Checklist and Notes for Pecos River Assessment Reach # 3

PFC Lotic (Riparian) Standard Checklist

Name of Riparian Area: ___Pecos River within Pecos NHP___

Date: __7-8-2010__ Segment/Reach ID: __Reach #3 – Abandoned iron bridge to southern park boundary__

Miles: __approx. 1 stream mile__   Acres:_____

ID Team Observers: __Joel Wagner, Mike Martin, Yvonne Chauvin_____

Yes	No	N/A	HYDROLOGY
X			1) Floodplain above bankfull is inundated in "relatively frequent" events
		X	2) Where beaver dams are present they are active and stable
X			3) Sinuosity, width/depth ratio, and gradient are in balance with the landscape setting (i.e., landform, geology, and bioclimatic region)
X			4) Riparian-wetland area is widening or has achieved potential extent
X			5) Upland watershed is not contributing to riparian-wetland degradation

Yes	No	N/A	VEGETATION
X			6) There is diverse age-class distribution of riparian-wetland vegetation (recruitment for maintenance/recovery)
X			7) There is diverse composition of riparian-wetland vegetation (for maintenance/recovery)
X			8) Species present indicate maintenance of riparian-wetland soil moisture characteristics
X			9) Streambank vegetation is comprised of those plants or plant communities that have root masses capable of withstanding high-streamflow events
X			10) Riparian-wetland plants exhibit high vigor
X			11) Adequate riparian-wetland vegetative cover is present to protect banks and dissipate energy during high flows
		X	12) Plant communities are an adequate source of coarse and/or large woody material (for maintenance/recovery)

Yes	No	N/A	EROSION/DEPOSITION
X			13) Floodplain and channel characteristics (i.e., rocks, overflow channels, coarse and/or large woody material) are adequate to dissipate energy
X			14) Point bars are revegetating with riparian-wetland vegetation
X			15) Lateral stream movement is associated with natural sinuosity
X			16) System is vertically stable
X			17) Stream is in balance with the water and sediment being supplied by the watershed (i.e., no excessive erosion or deposition)

(Revised 1999)

Remarks (numbers correspond to checklist items)

1. Two higher Quaternary terraces don't experience frequent flooding, however, the lowest terraces (which are relatively narrow) and point bars are frequently inundated.

3. Overall gradient strongly controlled by bedrock outcrops, but the meander belt is wide enough so that alluvial reaches exist between the bedrock-controlled segments, allowing for sequential cutbank/point bar morphology. Point bars are better developed here than on reaches 1 and 2, being larger in width and area and having more diverse topographic structure (including oxbows and shoot cutoffs). This contributes to the more diverse wetland-riparian vegetation communities discussed in 7. below.

6. On the 2nd terraces, narrow-leaf cottonwoods (*Populus angustifolia*) are spreading clonally to provide significant recruitment. On the lowest terraces and point bars, sandbar willows (*Salix exigua*) are spreading clonally to provide significant recruitment. Some young thinleaf alders (*Alnus incana* ssp. *tenuifolia*), strapleaf willows *(Salix ligulifolia)*, peachleaf willows *(Salix amygdaloides)* and cottonwoods, including a few Rio Grande cottonwoods *(Populus deltoides* ssp. *wislizeni*), are establishing on lower terraces/point bars. Herbaceous wetland species such as reed-canary grass *(Phalaris arundinacea)* form dense mats in the wetter locations.

7. Narrow-leaf cottonwoods and some Rocky Mountain junipers *(Juniperus scopulorum)* are found on the 2nd terraces. (There are some decadent cottonwoods, but not enough to raise concerns.) Box-elder *(Acer negundo)* is more common on this reach, but it is not a dominant. Sandbar willows dominate the lower terraces/point bars, with young thinleaf alders, strapleaf willows and peachleaf willows present (still scattered, but more frequent than in the other reaches). Saplings of both cottonwood species are present, especially on active floodplain features with diverse structure. Through much of the reach, reed-canary grass and spikerush *(Eleocharis* sp.*)* are the dominant herbaceous wetland species within the active floodplain. However, the greater diversity of floodplain structural components on the large point bars (e.g., overflow channels, abandoned meanders) provides habitat for dense patches of arctic rush *(Juncus arcticus)*, Nebraska sedge *(Carex nebrascensis)*, cattail *(Typha* sp.*)*, redtop *(Agrostis gigantea)*, and several other *Carex* and *Juncus* species. A Huron green orchid *(Platanthera huronensis)* and patches of non-native teasel *(Dipsacus* sp.*)* were also observed on low terraces/pointbars. Grass cover on the 2nd terraces is almost entirely non-native.

13. Broad meanders allow formation of shoot cutoffs during overbank flows. Some of the bedrock outcrops encourage formation of mid-channel bars due to expansion, further dissipating energy.

15. The larger point bars include abandoned channels (oxbows).

16. Gradient is strongly controlled by substantial bedrock outcrops.

Summary Determination

Functional Rating:

Proper Functioning Condition	__X__
Functional – At Risk	_____
Nonfunctional	_____

Trend for Functional – At Risk:

Upward	_____
Downward	_____
Not Apparent	_____

Note: <u>Observations regarding fishing impacts</u>: No evidence of trailing, localized vegetation trampling, bank destabilization or trash observed.

Are factors contributing to unacceptable conditions outside the control of the manager?
Yes ___ No __X__

If yes, what are those factors?

___ Flow regulations	___ Mining activities	___ Upstream channel conditions
___ Channelization	___ Road encroachment	___ Oil field water discharge
___ Augmented flows	___ Other (specify)	

32

Appendix 4. PFC Riparian System Standard Checklist and Notes for Glorieta Creek Assessment Reach

PFC Lotic (Riparian) Standard Checklist

Name of Riparian Area: ___Glorieta Creek within Pecos NHP_____

Date: __7-8-2010_____ Segment/Reach ID: _Highway 63 bridge downstream to lower end of remaining artificial levee (0.5 stream miles below bridge)

Miles: _approx. 0.5 stream miles___ Acres:_____

ID Team Observers: _Joel Wagner, Mike Martin, Yvonne Chauvin_____

Yes	No	N/A	HYDROLOGY
X			1) Floodplain above bankfull is inundated in "relatively frequent" events
X			2) Where beaver dams are present they are active and stable
	X		3) Sinuosity, width/depth ratio, and gradient are in balance with the landscape setting (i.e., landform, geology, and bioclimatic region)
	X		4) Riparian-wetland area is widening or has achieved potential extent
X			5) Upland watershed is not contributing to riparian-wetland degradation

Yes	No	N/A	VEGETATION
X			6) There is diverse age-class distribution of riparian-wetland vegetation (recruitment for maintenance/recovery)
X			7) There is diverse composition of riparian-wetland vegetation (for maintenance/recovery)
X			8) Species present indicate maintenance of riparian-wetland soil moisture characteristics
X			9) Streambank vegetation is comprised of those plants or plant communities that have root masses capable of withstanding high-streamflow events
X			10) Riparian-wetland plants exhibit high vigor
X			11) Adequate riparian-wetland vegetative cover is present to protect banks and dissipate energy during high flows
		X	12) Plant communities are an adequate source of coarse and/or large woody material (for maintenance/recovery)

Yes	No	N/A	EROSION/DEPOSITION
X			13) Floodplain and channel characteristics (i.e., rocks, overflow channels, coarse and/or large woody material) are adequate to dissipate energy
X			14) Point bars are revegetating with riparian-wetland vegetation
	X		15) Lateral stream movement is associated with natural sinuosity
X			16) System is vertically stable
X			17) Stream is in balance with the water and sediment being supplied by the watershed (i.e., no excessive erosion or deposition)

(Revised 1999)

Remarks (numbers correspond to checklist items)

2. Two beaver dams and associated ponds were observed in sequence at approximately 0.27 and 0.35 stream miles below the Highway 63 bridge. Both are well-stabilized by riparian shrubs and are being actively maintained (beaver observed in upper pond).
3. Levee on east and south side of former "upper reservoir" (built in mid 1980s and left in place during 1999-2000 lower Glorieta Creek restoration project) confines channel. Channel is forced to stay within an artificially narrow meander belt between the levee and the high terrace to the south (gradient steepens due to reduced sinuosity).
4. Levee described above restricts potential width of riparian area.
6/7. Middle-aged trees and saplings of Rio Grande cottonwood (*Populus deltoides* ssp. *wislizeni*) provide appropriate age-classes for riparian trees along entire reach. Scattered narrow-leaved cottonwoods (*Populus angustifolia*) present in upper part of reach, but become more common near lower end of the levee, and are spreading clonally. Seedlings and saplings of both cottonwood species are common w/in footprint of the restored "upper reservoir" site. Sandbar willow (*Salix exigua*) is the dominant shrub throughout the active floodplain and is spreading clonally to provide significant recruitment. Dewystem willow (*Salix irrorata*) well-represented and most are young, indicating ongoing recruitment. Arctic rush (*Juncus arcticus*), spikerush (*Eleocharis sp.*), common three-square (*Schoenoplectus pungens*), cattail (*Typha latifolia*) and Nebraska sedge (*Carex nebrascensis*) form dense mats w/in the active floodplain (and w/in the restored "upper reservoir"). Non-native grasses on drier terraces include tall fescue (*Festuca arundinacea*) and Kentucky bluegrass (*Poa pratensis*).
14. A very large, structurally complex and well-vegetated point bar exists in the upper half of this reach. Point bar development is constrained by the artificial levee in the lower half of the reach, but would be free to develop to potential size and structural complexity over time if the levee was removed.
15. Artificial levee constrains lateral stream movement and reduces sinuosity (see 3. above).

Summary Determination

Functional Rating:

Proper Functioning Condition	____
Functional – At Risk	__X__
Nonfunctional	____

Trend for Functional – At Risk:

Upward	____
Downward	__X__
Not Apparent	____

Notes: Remaining portion of the artificial levee (west and south sides of the old upper reservoir) limits potential for lateral stream migration across the valley floor. This constriction limits the development of riparian area size, structural complexity and habitat diversity. At this time, the channel and floodplain adjacent to levee appear to function properly despite the constriction, and the channel doesn't appear to be susceptible to excessive erosion or incision in large storms. However, the levee poses a risk of excessive sediment contributions to downstream aquatic systems if a large storm causes the creek to erode a new channel through the levee (lower beaver dam is most likely location for levee failure) and down through the restored wetland area. Trend is downward because the levee will continue to degrade over time, increasing chances for failure. We recommend complete removal of the levee to restore the riparian-wetland landscape, allow the riparian zone to reach its full potential for size and habitat diversity, and eliminate the potential for excessive sediment deposition in downstream aquatic systems.

Are factors contributing to unacceptable conditions outside the control of the manager?
Yes ____ No __X__

If yes, what are those factors?

____ Flow regulations	____ Mining activities	____ Upstream channel conditions
____ Channelization	____ Road encroachment	____ Oil field water discharge
____ Augmented flows	____ Other (specify)	

NPS 430/108149, July 2011